The Live More Journal

— .. —

52 Prompts to Help You Learn About & Love Yourself

The Live More Journal: 52 Prompts to Help You Learn About and Love Yourself
© 2015 by Nicole Liloia International

For print or media interviews with Nicole, please contact nicole@nicoleliloia.com

First Printing, 2015

ISBN 978-0692595947

www.nicoleliloia.com

Introduction

If you've ever stopped and wondered "Who am I?" or "What do I want my life to be about?" then you're in the right place! I wrote this book to help you figure that out so you can worry less and live more. If you had asked me what I really wanted my life to be like and what was important to me back when I was operating on autopilot all the time, I'm not sure I would have been able to tell you. I probably would have said I was too busy to even think about it.

I actually learned strategies to become more present and manage my stress so I was able to change my habits and learn to enjoy life as it was happening. This also helped me figure out what I really wanted to make my life about and that wasn't working all the time or worrying about what could go wrong next. I wish that I had been given an opportunity sooner to figure out who I really was and what was holding me back from the success that I wanted.

I've created these journal prompts for you so that you can take some time to slow down and think about what's important to you. These prompts will inspire you to think more about your life and experiences and give you some clarity on what you want your life to be about right now. The best part is that you can have fun with this process as there are no right or wrong answers for these questions. Just let your thoughts flow as you write and you'll be able to really dig deep and learn more about yourself!

Warmly,

The Benefits of Journaling

These journal prompts are actually designed to help you learn about yourself and love yourself more. Once you understand yourself better, you won't be judgmental about the choices you've made in your life and you'll appreciate yourself more. Some of the other benefits that journaling can provide you as well include:

- Increases your ability to focus
- Enhances your creativity
- Gives you a way to express yourself
- Helps you to process and let go of past experiences
- Provides you with insight into your desires and plans for the future
- Helps you to discover solutions to problems you're experiencing
- Teaches you how to write stories
- Is a self-care ritual
- Allows you to identify your strengths
- Reduces stress through the release of negative emotions
- Helps you to improve your writing skills

Ready to get started with journaling and enjoy these benefits? Let's go!

How To Use These Journal Prompts

Honestly, there is no "right" way to use these journal prompts or journal, but if you're like me you want some guidance on the process. These steps will allow you to have the best experience possible from this workbook. Turn this process into a self-care ritual by making it relaxing and enjoyable.

Here are the steps to do that:

1. Get comfortable. Cuddle up in your favorite nook, sit in a cozy chair, or get comfy with a blanket. You want to be somewhere where you're able to write comfortably.

2. Light your favorite candle. You know the one – you've been saving it for a special occasion and this is it.

3. Treat yourself a cup of your favorite tea (or coffee) while you write.

4. If you're writing this out by hand, use a colored pen – whatever color is relaxing or makes you happy.

5. Turn off all distractions so that you're 100% focused on what you're thinking and writing about. That means no TV and no e-mail during this time. These prompts are giving you the opportunity to get know yourself better so you might as well turn it into a date for yourself!

There are 52 journal prompts in this book so that you can do one journal entry each week for the next year. Of course, you're welcome to go through them more quickly or slowly if you choose. They're not in any special order so you can jump around the book if you choose. I do suggest if you get to one that seems difficult to answer or makes you think "I don't know" that you tackle it right then and there rather than passing it over for another time. There will be no better time. Some of these questions will challenge you to really think about experiences in your life, goals you have, and sometimes even make you deal with uncomfortable thoughts or feelings.

There's no specific amount of time you should spend writing out these journal entries and there's no specific length that they should be, either. You may have more to write for some questions then you do for others. Each prompt is on it's own page so that there's space for you to write out your journal entry right underneath it. You might even choose to get a separate journal and write out the prompts and your journal entries in there. Make this process as enjoyable and easy as possible for yourself.

I'm excited to hear about your experiences with these prompts!
Please feel free to e-mail me at nicole@nicoleliloia.com to share what you've learned about yourself.

1

Write about the best day of your life.

What did you do? Who was a part of it? What feelings did you experience that day? What happens in your body now when you remember it? How can you experience some of those feelings this week?

2

Think about a time that you handled a tough situation well.

What happened? How did you deal with it? Who offered you support during that time? How do you feel now when you think about this situation?

What do you really love about your work?

What goals do you want to achieve in your career? Do you want to be challenged? Do you want to feel comfortable? What's the one thing you wish was different about the work you do? What kind of changes can you make so your work is more enjoyable?

Write about a memory that you would like to let go of.

What happened? It may be an embarrassing situation, an argument with someone close to you, or even a loss you experienced. How do you feel when you think about the situation? How will you feel if you let go of this memory and not allow it to have any power over you?

What would you do if you never had to worry about money?

How does money limit you in your life right now? What are you beliefs about money that you want to change?

A genie grants you 3 wishes so you can have anything you want (except unlimited money).

What do you wish for? How would your life be different if those wishes came true? What steps can you take now to make those wishes come true?

Practicing gratitude is a powerful way to improve our mood and feel happy.

How do you know you are grateful for something? Create a list of 10 things you're grateful for right now. What kind of sensations do you experience in your body when you feel grateful? Is there a gratitude ritual that you would like to practice daily?

Describe what your ideal day would be like.

What time would you wake up? Where would it take place? What kind of activities would you do? Who would be a part of it? When can you have a day like this happen?

If you could meet anyone in the world, who would you choose?

What would you ask them and talk to them about? What would you feel like before meeting them? How do you think you would feel after the experience?

10

Write about the hardest day of your life – What happened?

Who was a part of it? What feelings did you experience that day? What happens in your body now when you remember it?

Write a letter to someone who you need to forgive.

What happened? Why are you choosing to forgive them? How do you feel when you think about forgiving them? How will your relationship be different when you've forgiven them?

12

If you could change one thing about your life, what would it be?

Why do you think that needs to be changed? How would you feel if the change happened? What's preventing you from making that change right now?

Where would you live if you could live anywhere that you wanted?

If you're living in your dream location, describe what exactly makes it that. If you would choose to live somewhere different, describe it. What would your home be like? What would the area be like? What would make it your ideal living space?

14

Write a love letter to yourself.

What do you love about yourself? What are your best traits? What are you proud of yourself for? We're all special — what makes you feel that way?

Write about your bad habits.

What habits do you have that block you from getting what you want? Do any of them prevent you from being successful? Have you tried to change these habits in the past? What can you do to change them right now?

What do you feel is the best advice you could ever give someone?

How did you learn this? Why do you feel it's such important advice? Who would you want to share this advice with?

17

Write a journal entry that takes place one year in the future.

What is your life like at this time? Where are you living? Who are the important people in your life? What kind of work are you doing? Is anything the same as it is right now? What changes have you made over the next year?

Write about a time that you remember feeling safe and protected in your life.

What makes you feel safe? Are there people who help you to feel this way? Is feeling safe important to you?

What is one decision you made that you wish you could have done differently?

How would you change that decision if you could? What happened as a result of the decision you chose? What do you think would have happened if you made the decision differently?

20

What message do you want to share with the world?

Why is it important that you share this message? What steps can you take to get this message out to people?

21

Write about your worries.

What keeps you up at night and unable to go to sleep? How do you feel when you think about these worries? What would help you to feel better about your worries?

Write a letter to someone who has had a big influence on your life but doesn't know it.

This can be someone who you've never met. How have the influenced your life?
What do you want to say to them about their influence on your life?

Write about a goal that you have reached and feel amazing about.

How did you decide that this is a goal that you wanted to achieve? What steps did you take to reach it? How have you celebrated reaching this goal? How do you feel when you think about this achievement?

Write about the self-care activities that you enjoy doing.

What do you do to take care of yourself and how do you feel before and after you do them? How did you discover that these activities made you feel good? If you don't participate in self-care activities, write about activities that make you feel good and how they can become a regular part of your self-care routine.

25

If you were to write a book, what would it be about?

Why would you choose that topic? Who would be the ideal audience to read your book? How do you feel when you think about writing this book?

What does the word "abundance" mean to you?

Do you have abundance in your life or do you want more of it? What steps can you take to feel more abundant? What would it mean for you to feel abundant in your life?

Write about your family.

What is your role within your family system? What is your favorite memory of spending time with them? What do you love about your family members? What do you wish was different about your family?

Write about what makes you angry.

When was the last time you got angry? What do you feel in your body when you think about being angry? How do you usually do with your feelings of anger?

Complete this sentence

_____ makes me happy.

What is it about this that makes you happy? How can you tell you're experiencing happiness? How often do you experience happiness and acknowledge it?

Write about a time you were surprised.

How did you feel about being surprised? Was there anything about it that made you uncomfortable? Do you wish to be surprised again?

What is something you want to do by your next birthday?

Why did you choose this? What are the steps you need to take to make it happen? How will you feel when you accomplished this?

Describe your dream vacation.

Where would you go and why? Would you travel by yourself or with someone? How long would you want to go away for? How would you feel at the end of the vacation?

Imagine that you were given $100,000 to donate however you wanted.

Where would you choose to donate the money? Why did you make this choice?
What would it feel like for you to donate that money?

Write about something you do really well.

Don't be afraid to brag! How do you know this is something you do really well?
How do you feel when you're doing this? What do you like about it?

35

What book or movie has had a really big impact on you?

How has it impacted your life? Did it have any influence on any decisions that you've made?

What is the biggest source of stress in your life right now?

How does it affect you? How do you deal with stress? What are 3 steps you can take to make this situation less stressful?

Who do you talk to when you have a problem?

Why do you choose this person? How do you feel when you're confiding in them? How do you feel after you've talked to them about it?

Describe your relationship with money.

What are some of the beliefs you grew up with about making money? Do you feel limited in how much you can make? When you think about money, what kind of sensations do you experience in your body?

Describe a situation that's been happening in your life that you have no control over.

How does the lack of control make you feel? Is there anything that you can do to regain control over the situation? How does lack of control cause you to feel in your body?

Write about a superpower that you would choose if you could have one.

What kind of things would you do with that superpower? Why did you choose this superpower? Do you think having a superpower would improve your life?

Write about a fear that you have overcome.

How did that fear impact your life? What steps did you take to get past this fear? How do you feel now when you think about that fear?

Write about a time that you felt "left out."

What did you do about it? How do you feel now when you think about that time? Do you wish did anything differently in dealing with that situation?

Write about someone you really admire.

What characteristics do you most admire about them? Do you have any of those same characteristics as them? Do you want to develop any of the those characteristics?

Write about something that you want to learn how to do.

Why do you want to learn this? How can you acquire this new skill? Would learning this skill improve your life? Describe what would be different.

How do you feel about fame and celebrities?

Would you ever want to be a celebrity? If you were a celebrity, what would you want to be known for? What do you think would be the best and worst parts of being a celebrity?

Who is somebody that you're jealous of?

Why do you feel jealous of them? What thoughts come up for you when you think about jealousy? What kind of feelings in your body does jealousy bring up for you?

Describe what you think your life will be like 10 years in the future.

Is this what you want your life to be like? What is a part of your life now that you still want to be a part of your life in 10 years?

How has technology affected your life?
(e.g. computers, internet, cell phones)

Is it an important part of your life? Do you wish you spent more or less time using it? How has it affected your relationships with others?

What are your biggest distractions?

What prevents you from accomplishing the things that you want to? How do you feel when you waste time instead of completing something that you're working on? How do you get your focus back?

Describe a situation that has been going on in your life that you have no control over.

How does the lack of control make you feel? Is there anything that you can do to regain control over the situation? How does lack of control cause you to feel in your body?

51

What was your favorite part of your childhood?

Was it a relationship with someone or an experience you had or something else? How does it make you feel when you think about it? Is there anything in your life today that brings up similar feelings for you?

Write about what your life is like in the present moment.

What do you love to spend time doing? Who is an important part of your life? What kind of work do you choose to do? What makes you happiest?

About Nicole

Nicole Liloia, LCSW helps smart-yet-stressed women make money doing work they love so that they can enjoy successful lifestyles now instead of waiting for "someday."

As a (former) stress addict + city girl (NYC to be exact), she knows what it's like to live a hectic, go go go lifestyle and feel like you're not truly alive because you're busy all the time. She quit the 9-5 world after her first full-time job and has been creating success on her own terms since then.

She's made it her mission to help women slow down, figure out what truly matters to them, and reclaim their lives.

Nicole has a Master's in Social Work from Columbia University in NYC and is a coach + business strategist, therapist, and writer. She helps her clients kick stress to the curb and create successful lifestyles so that they can experience more freedom, fun, and happiness now instead of someday.

Learn more about working with her at www.NicoleLiloia.com.

Want to share your journaling experience with Nicole? Or just say hi? Reach out to her at nicole@nicoleliloia.com

Want to know where to find me?

I'd love to hear from you, so don't forget to reach out!

🌐 www.nicoleliloia.com

✉ nicole@nicoleliloia.com

f facebook.com/liloia.nicole

🐦 @nicoleliloia

📷 @nicoleliloia

Featured In. . .

MindBodyGreen.com   SHEKNOWS

Forbes      Daily Parent

+ PositivityDaily   PurposeFairy    tiny buddha® simple wisdom for complex lives